P9-CCI-408

In Your Face
Poems About Real Life

In Your Face
Poems About Real Life

Tina Posner, Editor

SCHOLASTIC INC.
New York Toronto London Auckland Sydney
Mexico City New Delhi Hong Kong Buenos Aires

**Cover illustration
Luis Bueno, 17**

**The editors would like to thank the following students for their
invaluable input during the selection process:**

*Brandon Atkison
Kristina C. Grimm
Christopher Pollard
Tara Whittington*

Acknowledgments appear on pages 62–63, which constitute an extension
of this copyright page.

No part of this publication may be reproduced in whole or in part, or stored in a retrieval
system, or transmitted in any form or by any means, electronic, mechanical, photocopying,
recording, or otherwise, without written permission of the publisher. For information
regarding permission, write to Scholastic Inc., 557 Broadway, New York, NY 10012.

Compilation copyright © 2002 by Scholastic Inc.
All rights reserved. Published by Scholastic Inc.
Printed in the United States of America CGB

ISBN 0-439-12383-6
(meets NASTA specifications)

SCHOLASTIC, READ 180, and associated logos and designs are
trademarks and/or registered trademarks of Scholastic Inc.

LEXILE is a registered trademark of MetaMetrics, Inc.

10 11 12   12 11 10

Contents

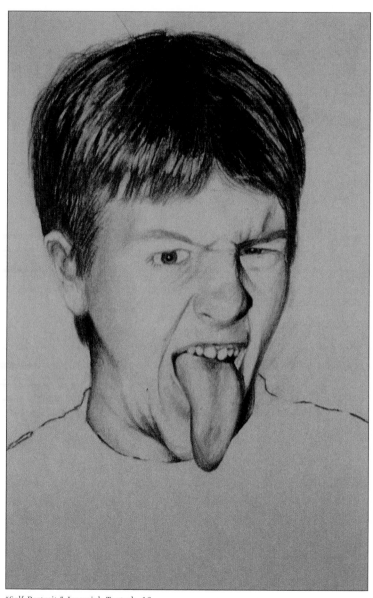

"Self-Portrait," Jeremiah Teutsch, 18

Introduction

If you think poetry equals corny . . . If you think poems were all written a long time ago . . . If you think poems have to rhyme and have to involve flowers in some way . . . Then, think again. This book contains poems that will change your mind. This book contains the poetry of today.

But let's back up for a second. What exactly *is* a poem? A poem is an expression of something important, usually using as few words as possible. Other than that, poetry is kind of hard to define.

It used to be easier. Back in the day, all poems had set patterns. It wasn't a poem if it didn't have a pattern of rhymes and a predictable rhythm.

Times have changed. Today, almost anything can be considered a poem. Poems don't have to rhyme. Poems don't even need to have line breaks. Just about any piece of writing can be called a poem.

Right now, poetry is everywhere. It's in homes on refrigerator magnets and on MTV. It's even happening in big-city nightclubs. Clubs are holding poetry competitions called slams. A slam is a loud and in-your-face contest to see who can do the best performance of a poem. It's a lot more like a pro-wrestling match than a trip to the library.

One poet, Stephen Colman, who's no stranger to slam, wrote about his passion for poetry in "Wanna Hear A Poem." Here's an excerpt.

I wanna hear a poem
I wanna learn something
I didn't know
I wanna say "YES" at the end
because I'm sick of saying "so?"

I wanna hear a poem
about who you are
and what you think
And why you slam
*not a poem about my poem—cause I know
who I am.*

I wanna hear a
love poem a sad poem an I hate
   my dad poem
a dream poem an I'm not what I
   seem poem
an I need poem an I also bleed poem
an I'm alone poem an I can't find my
   home poem

I just wanna hear a poem!

And if you wanna hear a poem too, read on. Inside is poetry that rages, struts, and whispers in your ear. Some of the poems were shouted out on stage at slams. Others were quietly scribbled on notebook pages. But all of them are guaranteed to get right up in your face. All of these poems will jump off the page and grab you. And we promise: no rhymes about flowers!

So, go ahead. Hear a poem.

What You See

Are my clothes cool? Is my hair right? Is my house nice? We try not to care what others think. But deep down, most of us *do* care about how things appear to others.

These first three poems are all about appearances. Each poet has a different take on how we show who we are to the world. Each poem reveals the truth behind what you see.

"The Professional," James Gates, 16

"Self-Portrait," Kaloni Davidson, 17

Getting Ready

i'm the thousand-change girl, getting ready
for school, standing in my bedroom, ripping
pants and shirts from my body, trying
    dresses
and skirts. my father, at the bottom of
    the steps
is yelling, the bus is coming, here comes
    the bus.
i'm wriggling into jeans, zippers grinding
    their teeth,
buttons refusing their holes. my brother,
    dressed-in-five-
minutes, stands in the hallway, t-shirt and
    bookbag,
saying, what's the big problem. i'm kneeling
    in front
of the closet, foraging for that great-lost-
    other-shoe.
downstairs, my father offers advice. slacks,
    he's yelling,
just put on some slacks. i'm in the mirror
    matching

earrings, nervous fingers putting the back
    to the front.
downstairs the bus is fuming in the yard,
    farm kids
with cowlicks sitting in rows. everything's
    in a pile
on the floor. after school, mother will
    scream,
get upstairs and hang up that mess, but
    i don't care.
i'm the thousand-change girl, trotting
    downstairs now
looking good, looking ready for school.
    father,
pulling back from the steps with disgust,
    giving me
the once over, saying, is *that* what you're
    wearing.

Debra Marquart

☛ *Notice how this poet uses all lowercase letters and long, run-on sentences. These help give the impression that the narrator is in a hurry.*

He Shaved His Head

He shaved his head to release
his imagination.
He did it to get a tattoo on his shiny head.
He did it to lose his normality.
He did it to become a freak.
He did it because he was angry.
He did it to make people angry.
He did it for himself.

Rene Ruiz, 13

☛ *The poet repeats the phrase "He did it" several times. You can hear
the anger build with each repetition. Maybe "he" has been asked too
many times why he did this—and he's tired of it.*

White Lies

The lies I could tell,
when I was growing up—
light-bright, near-white,
high-yellow, red-boned
in a black place—
were just white lies.

I could easily tell the white folks
that we lived "uptown,"
not in that pink and green,
shantyfied, shot-gun section
along the tracks. I could act
like my homemade dresses
came straight out the window
of *Maison Blanche*. I could even
keep quiet, quiet as kept,
like the time a white girl said,
squeezing my hand, "now
we have three of us in our class."

But I paid for it every time
Mama found out. She laid her hands
on me, then washed out my mouth

with Ivory Soap. "This is to purify,"
she said, "and cleanse your lying tongue."
Believing that, I swallowed suds
thinking they'd work
from the inside out.

Natasha Trethewey

"Self-Portrait," Ida Tate, 17

☛ *Did you notice that the title of this poem has two meanings? The
narrator is telling so-called "white" (or harmless) lies about where
she lives and where she bought her clothes. And she's also lying by
staying silent and not correcting people who think she's white.*

Straight From the Heart

Ah . . . love. Love has probably inspired more poetry than any other feeling. You might even have a really mushy love poem tucked away in a secret drawer somewhere.

If you do, don't be embarrassed because you're not alone. There are enough love songs on the radio to convince you of that! People in love have just got to shout it out. The next three poems are all straight from the heart.

"Heart Works," Nicole Storrs, 16

Skin Games #2

Your
permanent
tan
this
winter
looks
so
great
against
white
snow.
Ski
with
me
this
afternoon,

then
sit
at
our
table
tomorrow
morning,
then
transfer
to
my
home
room,
then
tell
me

which
planet
you
come
from,
then
move
next
door.
Just
smile
and
move
next
door.
Please

smile
and
lean
your
dark
curls
into
my
nose,
then
simply
move
next
door
right
now.

Arnold Adoff

☛ *Did it take you a second to figure out how to read this poem—from top to bottom in columns? The poet may be suggesting that it is written in code to keep other people from reading it.*

Sweet

To kiss you was . . . Sweet.
The feel of your tongue on my teeth was
. . . Sweet.
Your lips against mine were . . . Sweet.
The way you moved your tongue in my
mouth was . . . Sweet (and it made me
shiver).
The force of your kiss took me and it was
. . . Sweet.
I had bruises on the inside of my mouth
for a week and it was . . . Sweet.
I was amazed by my first real kiss and it
was . . . Sweet.
I remember our lips meeting at a party,
Dane, and that was . . . Sweet.
Take all the kisses in your life and put
them on a tape. Plug yourself in. Never
push stop. Now, that would be . . . Sweet.

Mandy Foster, 17

☛ *Notice how an ordinary word like "sweet" takes on layers of meaning
through repetition.*

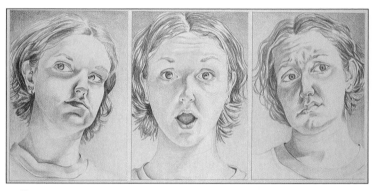

"Self-Portrait," Stacey Mairs, 17

Forever

You told me that we were going
to be together
forever.
You said that I was yours
and you were mine
forever.
You said that you were going
to love me
forever.
I wish you would have told me that
forever
is only
three months long.

Angela Shelf Medearis

☛ *Irony is when something turns out the opposite of how you expected.
In this poem, the irony is that "forever" turned out to be much shorter
than the narrator expected.*

Family Feeling

You can't live with them. You can't kick them out on the curb. They're your family. You didn't choose them, but you probably love them all the same.

Still, it isn't always easy. Sometimes moms are aggravating. Sometimes dads leave. Sometimes it's the other way around. And sometimes your parents act like the kids.

The next three poems confront the strain and affection that make up that family feeling.

"Untitled," Lesley McTague, 17

Last Photograph with My Father

Don't know how it all started. The frozen
     feeling,
this fender inside wanting to crash against
     everything.
Blown out blue night. My face.

That's me.
See the kid with a buzzed head.

Kinky overalls, bluish and acrylic spray
fat letters down the pants. Fists curled
like bike locks. Mama says, Don't be so
     angry.

Just making it up. I say.
Just making it up. In the kitchen with
     Selena on,
her hard black guitar eyes.

My eyes hard too. Like my father César's.
He's gone. With his new family in Denver.
Toña, Benita, his other kids.
Other wife, Olivia.

"Will," Jon Blank-Rosenblum, 17

Mama says *paciencia*[1]
   like she says go
    to your room.
I was born on the road.
   That's all I know.

Road of black starry grapes
waiting to crash,
that burn on wire vines.

Grapes pruned and pulled.
Grapes thrown cut and dropped dry.

☛ *Here, the narrator begins a flashback to a time when the family was together on a grape farm in Fowlerville. Notice how words like* crash, burn, fiery, *and* biting *reveal the narrator's anger.*

[1] patience

They dry in the fiery red dust of Fowlerville.
Fowlerville, say it out loud. Say it biting
   my lips.

Father carries me in his arms. A torn brown
photograph I keep on the wall.

Campesino[2] shirt blue,
our trailer in tin.

Don't lose this *foto*[3],
she tells me. Mama Lucy.
Back at the kitchen window.
   Apartment #9—
"C" Street, Westside *barrio*[4]. Stare with
   my hard eyes.
Out into the night. Disappear.

Juan Felipe Herrera

[2] farm worker
[3] photo
[4] neighborhood

Deformed Finger

Don't stick your finger in the ketchup bottle,
Mother said. It might get stuck, &
then you'll have to wait for your father
to get home to pull it out. He
won't be happy to find a dirty fingernail
squirming in the ketchup that he's going
   to use
on his hamburger. He'll yank it out so hard
that for the rest of your life you won't
be able to wear a ring on that finger.
And if you ever get a girlfriend, &
you hold hands, she's bound to ask you
why one of your fingers is deformed,
& you'll be obligated to tell her how
you didn't listen to your mother, &
insisted on playing with a ketchup bottle,
& she'll get to thinking, he probably won't
listen to me either, & she'll push your
   hand away.

Hal Sirowitz

☛ *This poet writes in the narrator's mother's voice, like a comedian
doing an impression.*

"Self-Portrait," Monica Simmons, 16

Wade's Hoggers

☛ *This poem is written as the narrator's stream-of-consciousness, or flow of thoughts, about the name of her mother's bowling team.*

The name of my mother's bowling team.

"You have to know what a hogger is," she
    said.

I'm thinking pig. Fat pigs.
I'm thinking it's not funny to name a team
    "Hoggers."
I'm thinking of the time I was nearly
    suspended
from fourth grade
for fighting with a girl
who said my mother was fat.

I'm thinking of how careful my mother was
to take dainty steps
and walk slowly
so that the wind was not disturbed by her
    mass,
so that people didn't get pushed over
by her wake.

I'm thinking about her shock
at the obvious disgust of my father
as she grew larger after every child.

I'm thinking of tropical purple mu mus
sagging chairs,
stretched-out shoes.

I'm thinking about her heart getting
    squeezed
between her lungs.

I'm thinking about a photo of my mother at
    age four.
Her chubby, baby-fat face,
her hands hooked in the front by two plump
    fingers,
she is standing in front of her house.
To her left is a table, and a cake with four
    candles.
She's not smiling.

"What is a hogger, mom?" I ask.

"It digs up potatoes. It's a farm tool."

"Oh," I say.

I'm thinking of Wade
hanging a framed photo of his champion
    Hoggers
on the wall of his shop.

I'm thinking of all the farmers who
will comment on the picture: a row of
    women in their fifties,
"Hoggers" stitched in pink across their
    chests.

I want to say, "Mom, eat the cake."

Debbra Palmer

☛ *In the last line, the narrator goes back to her mother's fourth-birthday photo. She seems to wish she could travel back in time and make her mother happy.*

The Pen Is Mightier

According to the old expression, "The pen is mightier than the sword." Or, to put it another way, words can be powerful weapons. So when something is just plain wrong and demands action, why not put pen to paper? Let people know what's up. Move mountains with your words.

That's what these poets did in the next three poems. They put their mighty pens to paper and spoke out against injustice.

"Self-Portrait," Jon Blank-Rosenblum, 17

"American Dream," Stephen Ludwig, 17

Bandaids and Five Dollar Bills

My students wrote essays for homework
    this week,
The usual stuff for grade ten,
I asked them to write how they'd change
    the world
If the changing was left up to them.

His name was Rick Johnson; he was surly
    and shy,
A student who's always ignored.
He'd slouch in his seat with a Malcolm X cap,
Half-sleep, making sure he looked bored.

His essay was late—just before I went home,
It was wrinkled and scribbled and thin,
I thought to reject it . . . (Why do teachers
    do that?)
But I thanked him for turning it in.

"You can't cure the world," his essay began,
"Of the millions of evils and ills,
But to clean up my world so I could survive,
I'd cut bandaids and five dollar bills.

"Now bandaids are beige—says right on
    the box
'Skin tone' is the color inside.
Whose skin tone? Not mine! Been lookin'
    for years
For someone with that color hide.

"Cause bandaids show up, looking pasty
    and pale,
It's hard to pretend they're not there,
When the old man has beat me and I gotta
    get stitches,
Them bandaids don't cover or care.

"And now, you may ask, why would
    anyone want
To get rid of five dollar bills?
Cause for just that much cash, a dude's
    mama can buy
A crack rock, or whiskey, or pills.

"She smokes it or drinks it, and screams at
    her kids,
Then passes out cold on the floor,
By morn she remembers no pain, just
    the void,
And her kids wish the world had a door.

"So my magical dream is not out of reach,
Like curing cancer or AIDS, or huge ills,
All I ask from my life is a little respect,
And no bandaids or five dollar bills."

Sharon M. Draper

☞ *In this poem, Band-Aids and five dollar bills are* symbols — *they
stand for the problems of racial prejudice, domestic violence, and
substance abuse.*

"Two Figures," Sarah Murphy, 16

Suspicion

A teenager—
Closely watched by store security
As to avoid any kind of larceny
Through his eyes, this kid is surely a thief.
He surveys her every move
Waiting for the act
So that he can catch her and set her straight.
Straight, unlike her tousled bright-red hair
He shakes his head in disapproval
Does she expect people not to stare?
Impossible

With her graffiti-colored,
Over-sized jeans; too-wide
black clunky boots; too high
topping it off, with nothing at all;
tiny tight shirt, much too small.
Thick silver chains,
her jewelry no doubt,

☛ *The poet uses lots of details about the teen's appearance to show how closely the guard is watching her.*

Make it easy to keep track of her
    whereabouts
Thanks to the annoying sound they chime

They look ridiculous, as though enslaving her,
Forcing her to go out in public as she does
And yet, she seems confident,
Proud of her image
Security guard wonders when she'll grow up
He paces back and forth—impatiently
As if waiting for her to make the change
to "maturity"
Before even exiting the store

An adult—
Walks by with grace and class
Lengthy blond, businesswoman in designer
    clothing
Avoiding eye contact,
Dodging shoppers,
Heading directly towards the back of the aisle

The security guard suddenly remembers his
    objective
And searches for a young girl who seems to
    have
cleverly slipped away
He listens for the sounds of the chains
But everything is instantly drowned out
By the noise of the alarm system
JUSTICE.
With a smirk of satisfaction, he turns to face
the scene, to catch a glimpse
of the culprit

And as she lowers her
    blond head
in shame,
The red-headed teenager
    pays for her
blue nail polish.

Renée Gauvreau

☞ *Notice how the poet uses only one physical detail to identify the
real shoplifter.*

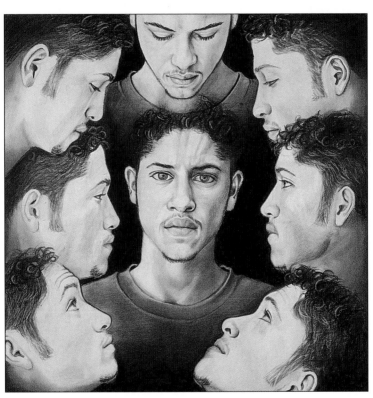

"Self-Portrait," Kevid Arias, 15

Blink Your Eyes

(Remembering Sterling A. Brown[1])

I was on my way to see my woman
but the Law said I was on my way
thru a red light red light red light
and if you saw my woman
you could understand.
I was just being a man.
It wasn't about no light
it was about my ride
and if you saw my ride
you could dig that too, you dig?
Sunroof stereo radio black
    leather
bucket seats sit low you
    know,
the body's cool, but the
    tires are worn.
Ride when the hard times
    come, ride

☛ *The narrator was feeling good, his car was cool, his date was hot, nothing was going to stop him—so he saw the light as green.*

[1] *an African-American poet and teacher*

when they're gone, in other words
the light was green.

I could wake up in the morning
without a warning
and my world could change:
blink your eyes.
All depends, all depends on the skin,
all depends on the skin you're living in

Up to the window comes the Law
with his hand on his gun
what's up? what's happening?
I said I guess
that's when I really broke the law.

He said *a routine, step
    out the car*
a routine, *assume the
    position.*
*Put your hands up in the air
you know the routine, like
    you just don't care.
License and registration.*
Deep was the night and the light

☛ *The words in italics
blend some of what
the police officer says
with what the narrator
imagines the police
officer is thinking.*

from the North Star on the car door, déjà vu
we've been through this before.
why did you stop me?
Somebody had to stop you.
I watch the news, you always lose.
You're unreliable, that's undeniable.
This is serious, you could be dangerous.

I could wake up in the morning
without a warning
and my world could change:
blink your eyes.
All depends, all depends on the skin,
all depends on the skin you're living in
New York City, they got laws
can't no bruthas drive outdoors,
in certain neighborhoods, on particular
    streets
near and around certain types of people.
They got laws.
All depends, all depends on the skin
all depends on the skin you're living in.

Sekou Sundiata

Who Am I?

"Who Am I?" is a question we begin asking as adolescents and keep asking our whole lives. How do you define yourself—by your heritage, your neighborhood, or your personality? And how would you describe your personality, anyway?

It is one of the great struggles of humanity—to understand who we are. That's why identity is one of poetry's most popular subjects. Each of these last three poems attempts to answer the question "Who Am I?"

"Disheveled," Lauren Wolff, 18

Super Girl

I used to be a super girl.
Everybody said so.
Leapt tall buildings in a single bound
and always said
thank you to my
elders.
Carried bags for people
who couldn't
and saved cats out
of trees on bright
summer days.
Always brushed my teeth after meals too
'cause the super girl manual said so.
But it's hard staying a super girl.
And sometimes no good deed goes
    unpunished.
I used to be a super girl.

Angela Johnson

☛ *Notice how super powers are included along with the narrator's ordinary efforts. This exaggeration helps give you a sense of how hard she tried to be good.*

☛ *The narrator doesn't really explain why she stopped being a super girl. She leaves it for you to imagine. But here's a clue: "no good deed goes unpunished." What do you think she means?*

"Self-Portrait II," Ida Tate, 17

Habits

We do have a few
 strange habits
in my family like the way
we fix corn on the cob.

☛ *The narrator only discusses one of his family's strange habits. But the title and the first line suggest that there are other strange habits.*

First we butter a slice of
 white bread
and fold it around the corn hot-dog style.

Trust me: you won't find a better way
to get your corn nice and melty
(plus you get to eat the bread).

At restaurants we have to fix our corn
like all the other normal families
using knives to spread the butter

every one of us secretly
 wishing for
slices of white buttered
 bread
so we can do it right.

☛ *Because the narrator describes his family's habits with humor—not anger or regret—the reader knows that he really enjoys being a member of this family.*

Ralph Fletcher

Notes for a Poem
on Being Asian American

As a child, I was a fussy
	eater
and I would separate the
	yolk from the egg white
as I now try to sort out
	what is Asian
in me from what is
	American—
the east from the west, the
	dreamer from the
	dream.
But countries are not
like eggs—except in the
	fragileness
of their shells—and eggs
	resemble countries
only in that when you
	crack one open and
	look inside,
you know even less than
	when you started.

☛ *The narrator describes
the difficult process
of separating an egg
as a metaphor for
(or symbol for) his
attempts to separate
his Asian-ness from
his American-ness.*

"Divided Culture," Boris Chang, Jr., 17

And so I crack open the egg,
and this is what I see:
two moments from my past that
    strike me
as being uniquely Asian American.

In the first, I'm walking down
    Michigan Avenue
one day—a man comes up to me out
    of the blue and says:
"I just wanted to tell you . . .
    I was on the plane that
bombed Hiroshima[1]. And I just wanted
    you to know that
what we did was for the good of
    everyone." And it
seems as if he's asking for my
    forgiveness. It's 1983,
there's a sale on Marimekko sheets at
    the Crate &

---

[1] *In 1945, the United States dropped atomic bombs on the Japanese cities of Hiroshima and Nagasaki. Approximately 140,000 people were killed. Japan then surrendered, ending World War II.*

Barrel, it's a beautiful summer day and
    I'm talking to
a man I've never seen before and will
    probably never
see again. His statement has no
    connection to me—
and has every connection in the world.
    But it's not
for me to forgive him. He must
    forgive himself.
"It must have been a very difficult
    decision to do what
you did," I say and mention the sale
    on Marimekko
sheets across the street, comforters,
    and how the
pillowcases have the pattern of wheat
    printed on them,
and how some nights if you hold them
    before an open
window to the breeze, they might
    seem like flags—

like someone surrendering after a great
    while, or
celebrating, or simply cooling
    themselves in the summer
breeze as best they can.

In the second moment—I'm in a taxi
    and the Iranian
cabdriver looking into the rearview
    mirror notices my
Asian eyes, those almond shapes,
    reflected in the glass
and says, "Can you really tell the
    difference between
a Chinese and a Japanese?"

And I look at his 3rd World face, his
    photo I.D. pinned
to the dashboard like a medal, and I
    think of the eggs
we try to separate, the miles from
    home he is and the
minutes from home I am, and I want
    to say: "I think

it's more important to find the
    similarities between
people than the differences." But
    instead I simply
look into the mirror, into his beautiful
    3rd World
eyes and say, "Mr. Cabdriver, I can
    barely tell the
difference between you and me."

Dwight Okita

☛ *The narrator seems to conclude that there's more connecting*
Americans — no matter what their ethnicity — than separating them.

Get Busy

So, now that you've read some poetry by other people, here are some ideas to help you create your own. Stay loose and have fun.

1. **Acrostic:** Write a word (for example, your name) down the left side of a page. Start each line with a letter from that word.

2. **Anagram:** Write out your whole name. Mix up the letters. How many different words can you make? Use these words to write a poem about yourself.

3. **Cut Up:** Take a newspaper or magazine article and cut it up into lines, phrases or words. (You can use more than one article, if you want.) Put the pieces of paper in a bag and pull them out at random.

4. **Rhyming Simon:** List five words. Now think of a rhyme for each of them. Then use these words to create a ten-line poem.

5. **Snapshot:** Write a poem that takes an imaginary snapshot of someone or something. Avoid common descriptions, such as: "The sky was gray." Instead, describe your own way of seeing things, for example: "The sky was the color of a dirty rag."

6. **Dream Weaver:** Tell the story of a dream or use images from a dream you can remember.

7. **Spy Cam:** Go outside and collect words and phrases from your neighborhood: street signs, advertisements, snatches of conversation, the words from a song. Use what you collect to write a poem.

8. **Recipe:** Make a recipe for something that has nothing to do with food, such as a recipe for *fun*. For example, "Take a heaping cup of friends, add a tablespoon of laughter and a pinch of screaming, mix well on a roller coaster . . . ."

9. **Remember When:** Write about a memory, but pretend it happened to someone else.

10. Feeling Entitled: First, choose a title. It could be any word or phrase that you think sounds interesting or funny, like "My Cat Has Bad Habits" or "If My Shoes Could Talk." Then write a poem that goes with that title.

"Self-Portrait in Doorknob," Maximilian Schubert, 17

Acknowledgments

Excerpt from "Wanna Hear A Poem" by Stephen Colman from BURNING DOWN THE HOUSE. Copyright © 2000 by Stephen Colman. Published by Soft Skull Press, Inc. Reprinted by permission of the author. All rights reserved.

"Getting Ready" by Debra Marquart from THE PARTY TRAIN, edited by Robert Alexander, Mark Vinz, and C. W. Truesdale. Copyright © 1996 by Debra Marquart. Published by New Rivers Press. Reprinted by permission of the author. All rights reserved.

"He Shaved His Head" by Rene Ruiz from YOU HEAR ME?, edited by Betsy Franco. Copyright © 2000 by Rene Ruiz. Published by Candlewick Press. Reprinted by permission of the author. All rights reserved.

"White Lies" by Natasha Trethewey from TWO WORLDS WALKING, edited by Diane Glancy and C. W. Truesdale. Copyright © 1994 by Natasha Trethewey. Published by New Rivers Press. Reprinted by permission of the author. All rights reserved.

"Skin Games #2" from SLOW DANCE HEART BREAK RULES by Arnold Adoff. Text copyright © 1995 by Arnold Adoff. Reprinted by permission of HarperCollins Publishers. All rights reserved.

"Sweet" by Mandy Foster from THE PAIN TREE AND OTHER TEENAGE ANGST-RIDDEN POETRY, collected by Esther Pearl Watson and Mark Todd. Copyright © 2000 by Mandy Foster. Published by Houghton Mifflin Co. Reprinted by permission of the author. All rights reserved.

"Forever" from SKIN DEEP AND OTHER TEENAGE REFLECTIONS by Angela Shelf Medearis. Text copyright © 1995 by Angela Shelf Medearis. Reprinted by permission of Diva Productions, Inc. All rights reserved.

"Last Photograph with My Father" from CRASH BOOM LOVE by Juan Felipe Herrera. Copyright © 1999 by Juan Felipe Herrera. Reprinted by permission of University of New Mexico Press. All rights reserved.

"Deformed Finger" by Hal Sirowitz from ALOUD: VOICES FROM THE NUYORICAN POETS CAFE, edited by Miguel Algarín and Bob Holman. Copyright © 1994 by Hal Sirowitz. Originally appeared in "Hanging Loose." Reprinted by permission of Henry Holt and Company, Inc. All rights reserved.

"Wade's Hoggers" by Debbra Palmer from PRESENT TENSE, edited by Micki Reaman, Amy Agnello, et al. Copyright © 1996 by Debbra Palmer. Published by Calyx Books. Reprinted by permission of the author. All rights reserved.

"Bandaids and Five Dollar Bills" from BUTTERED BONES by Sharon M. Draper. Copyright © 1993 by Sharon M. Draper. Reprinted by permission of the author. All rights reserved.

"Suspicion" by Renée Gauvreau from CHICKEN SOUP FOR THE TEENAGE SOUL III. Copyright © 2000 by Renée Gauvreau. Published by Health Communications, Inc. Reprinted by permission of the author. All rights reserved.

"Blink Your Eyes" by Sekou Sundiata from WELCOME TO YOUR LIFE: WRITINGS FOR THE HEART OF YOUNG AMERICA, edited by David Haynes and Julie Landsman. Poem copyright © 1998 by Sekou Sundiata. Published by Milkweed Editions. Reprinted by permission of the author. All rights reserved.

"Super Girl" from RUNNING BACK TO LUDIE by Angela Johnson. Text copyright © 2001 by Angela Johnson. Published by Orchard Books. Reprinted by permission of Scholastic Inc. All rights reserved.

"Habits" from RELATIVELY SPEAKING: POEMS ABOUT FAMILY by Ralph Fletcher. Text copyright © 1999 by Ralph Fletcher. Published by Orchard Books. Reprinted by permission of Scholastic Inc. All rights reserved.

"Notes for a Poem on Being Asian American" from CROSSING WITH THE LIGHT by Dwight Okita. Copyright © 1992 by Dwight Okita. Published by Tia Chucha, Chicago, IL. Reprinted by permission of the author. All rights reserved.

Art Acknowledgments

Cover Illustration: Luis Bueno, 17, *Rubber Band Man,* Print, Gold Award, 2001, via SODA; **Page 6:** Jeremiah Teutsch, 18, *Self-Portrait,* Art Portfolio, The Portfolio Award, 2000, via SODA; **Page 11:** James Gates, 16, *The Professional,* Drawing, Pentad, 2001, via SODA; **Page 12:** Kaloni Davidson, 17, *Self-Portrait,* Drawing, American Visions Award, 2001, via SODA; **Page 17:** Ida Tate, 17, *Self-Portrait,* Painting, Gold Award, 2001, via SODA; **Page 19:** Nicole Storrs, 16, *Heart Works,* Ceramics, American Visions Award, 1999, via SODA; **Page 22:** Stacey Mairs, 17, *Self-Portrait,* Drawing, Gold Award, 2001, via SODA; **Page 25:** Lesley McTague, 17, *Untitled,* Art Portfolio, Binney & Smith Portfolio Series Second Prize, 1999, via SODA; **Page 27:** Jon Blank-Rosenblum, 17, *Will,* Art Portfolio, Drawing, The Portfolio Award, 2001, via SODA; **Page 30:** Monica Simmons, 16, *Self-Portrait,* Drawing, Gold Award, 2001, via SODA; **Page 35:** Jon Blank-Rosenblum, 17, *Self-Portrait,* Drawing, Art Portfolio, Drawing, The Portfolio Award, 2001, via SODA; **Page 36:** Stephen Ludwig, 17, *American Dream,* Photography, Pinnacle Award, 2001, via SODA; **Page 40:** Sarah Murphy, 16, *Two Figures,* Drawing, American Visions Award, 2001, via SODA; **Page 44:** Kevid Arias, 15, *Self-Portrait,* Drawing, American Visions Award, 2001, via SODA; **Page 49:** Lauren Wolff, 18, *Disheveled,* Art Portfolio, Binney & Smith Portfolio Series First Prize, 1999, via SODA; **Page 51:** Ida Tate, 17, *Self-Portrait II,* Drawing, Gold Award, 2000, via SODA; **Page 54:** Boris Chang, Jr., 17, *Divided Culture,* Art Portfolio, The Portfolio Award, 2001, via SODA; **Page 61:** Maximilian Schubert, 17, *Self-Portrait in Doorknob,* Drawing, Silver Award, 2001, via SODA